The Most Beautiful Women

LICHFIELD

THE MOST BEAUTIFUL WOMEN

CRESCENT BOOKS

New York

BROOKE SHIELDS

Aged, incredibly, sixteen years old, Brooke Shields is already a major film star — her most famous film to date being, probably, *Pretty Baby*. She has also starred in *The Blue Lagoon*, and *Endless Love* directed by Zeffirelli. Born in New York city she began modelling at the age of eleven months. Brooke is still at school and spends her time when not filming or causing a stir with controversial television advertisements for jeans, riding her thoroughbred horse and writing poetry.

Facing page: Princess Anne of Denmark

First published in Great Britain 1981
by Elm Tree Books/Hamish Hamilton Ltd
Garden House 57–59 Long Acre London WC2E 9JZ

Copyright © 1981 by Patrick Lichfield

Book design by Craig Dodd

This 1983 edition is published by
Crescent Books, distributed by Crown Publishers, Inc.

ISBN 0-241-517-423235

h g f e d c b a

Printed in Italy by Arnoldo Mondadori Editore, Verona

For My Mother

CONTENTS

ACKNOWLEDGEMENTS

The author would like to thank the following people and organizations for their help in the preparation of this book.

Avon, whose cosmetics were used for the majority of the photographs taken since this book was commissioned in 1980 and whose support of the whole project has been invaluable

Chalky Whyte, my assistant

Peter Kain, who printed the photographs

Anne Peto, for general research

Diana Davis, for the Californian research

Clayton Howard, make-up artist for the majority of the photographs

Annie Calvas-Blanchon for styling

Vidal Sassoon for hair-styling in London, New York and Paris

Terry Boxall

Joey Mills, who made-up Brooke Shields

Lichfield Laboratories and Ceta Colour Processing for the processing of colour work

Singapore Airlines for permission to reproduce a photograph commissioned by them

L'Oréal, for permission to reproduce a photograph commissioned by them

Browns of South Molton Street for the loan of clothes

Conde-Nast Publications, *Harpers & Queen, Queen*, the *Tatler*, the *Radio Times*, the *Sunday Times, Woman*, J. Walter Thompson Ltd., the *Telegraph Magazine, Fair Lady, Ritz* and the *National Enquirer* for permission to reproduce photographs commissioned by them.

John Whyte for the back jacket photograph

Every effort has been made to acknowledge all those who have helped me with this book but if there have been any omissions in this respect, we apologize and will be pleased to make the appropriate acknowledgement in any future editions.

FOREWORD

Anyone picking up this book might well say to themselves: 'Who on earth does he think he is to judge who are the most beautiful women. And why isn't so-and-so included?' The first point is less easily answered than the second. I have, during the years, amassed a very large collection of photographs, mostly of women, and the negatives now total over a million. During this time (and particularly as much of it was spent working for *Vogue* and other women's magazines), a great many undeniably beautiful women have sat for me and this has provided a marvellous foundation on which to build the rest of the material.

When I was commissioned to produce the book I set out, admittedly with some haste, to fill in the gaps. I travelled a good deal, often taking a flight to, say, Paris just to take one subject, but I could not be in more than one place at a time so there are, therefore, some omissions which may seem glaring. I deliberately did not chase people whom I did not want to photograph passionately and there were some people, perhaps, that I would like to have done years before but the opportunity never presented itself.

Thus this is very much a personal choice and my single regret is that there is room for only about half of those women whom I selected originally. Most of the women are internationally famous, names well known in every household and familiar from magazines, television and film screens. From my own photographs of these people I have selected those pictures that I hope reflect, not only their looks, but their personalities and also the pleasure a photographer has in setting, designing and posing a shot. A few of the names may not be familiar to you. In my travels I have photographed some women who, for one reason or another may never be famous, but whose sheer beauty justly merits their appearance in this book.

I am grateful to many people who have helped me to put this collection together; to the women who made it possible, and, most important, to Avon who provided the cosmetics used in the majority of the photographs taken since the book was commissioned and who have supported the project in every way from its inception.

I hope that this book will provide many hours of pleasure — almost as much as I have had in producing it.

SHUGBOROUGH
STAFFORD 1981

9

AVON
creates a world of beautiful women

Some women are born beautiful. Others become beautiful. At Avon, we've seen it happen millions of times in many different countries. We've seen women transform themselves from the people they appear to be, into the people they want to be.

Avon has been in the business of creating beautiful women for close on a hundred years. We've helped women make the most of themselves with our make-up. Our skin care. Our fragrances. Our fashion jewellery. And we've added the special relationship that comes with buying Avon from a Representative they know and trust, in the warmth of their own homes.

Some of the beautiful women Avon has created are in this book. Millions more are not. Their faces may not be so famous, but they're beautiful just the same. Helping them feel good, as well as look good, is our pleasure as well as our business. And thanks to them, Avon has become what it is today: the biggest name in the world for cosmetics, fragrances and fashion jewellery.

AVON
you've never looked so good

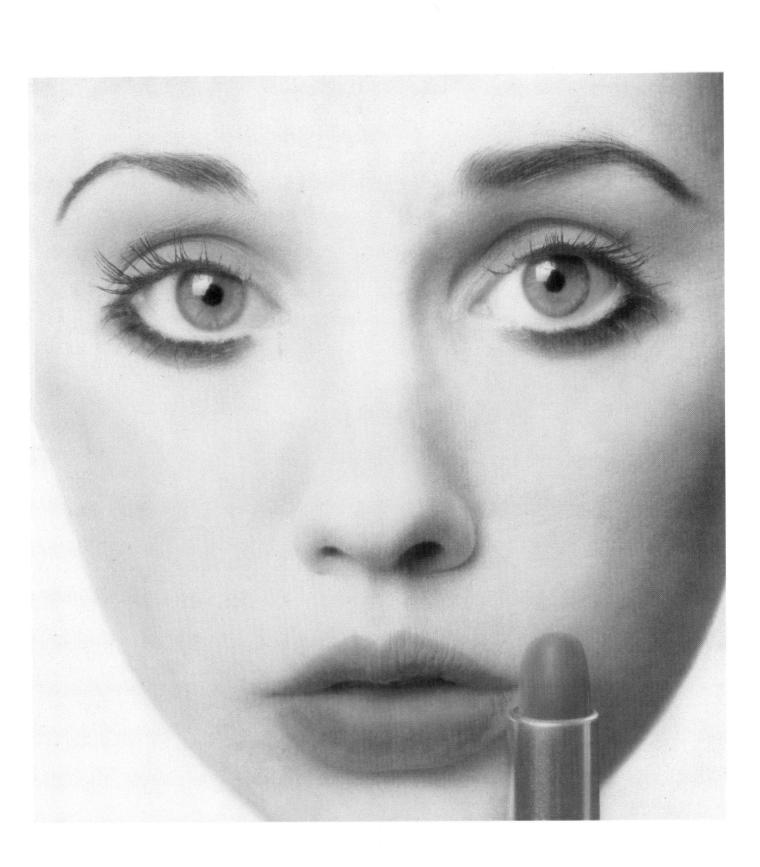

H.R.H. PRINCESS ALEXANDRA

Certainly one of the most popular members of the British Royal Family, Princess Alexandra inherited all the classic good looks of her mother, Princess Marina. Down-to-earth and full of charm she has an extraordinary ability to put people at their ease and, for all that she tends to avoid the limelight, these qualities are obviously part of the reason why she is so beloved by the public.

The success ratio of photography sessions with the Princess tends to be hampered by the fact that we are all laughing too much to concentrate. I have photographed her three times, in 1968, 74 and 80, each time to take the official pictures that have to be handed out when she is abroad on state visits.

THE DUCHESS OF WESTMINSTER

Tally Westminster married my brother-in-law, the Duke of Westminster — then Earl Grosvenor — when she was nineteen. This was an engagement picture, taken for *Vogue*, just before their wedding. Tally has the figure of a professional model, and natural elegance and grace, which makes her an easy subject for any photographer.

THE DUCHESS OF ROXBURGHE

At the risk of being accused of nepotism I include this shot of my sister-in-law, Jane Roxburghe. It was taken for *Tatler* as a cover photograph in 1978 and has a warmth that I like.

AUDREY HEPBURN

Elegant, gamine Hollywood star whose huge eyes, exquisite features and pencil-slimness have been appearing in marvellous films for nearly thirty years. Born in Belgium, of Irish-Dutch parentage, Audrey Hepburn has starred in films that have become part of Hollywood mythology: *Roman Holiday* (1953), *Funny Face* (1957), *The Nun's Story* (1959), *Breakfast At Tiffany's* (1961), *Charade* (1963), *My Fair Lady* (1964).

That her amazing face has survived the years not merely gracefully but with her very great beauty unimpaired can be seen from her role as Marian in the 1976 film, *Robin and Marian*.

This photograph was taken in Rome on a cold and sunny day in January 1981. It marked the ending of the book and it was perhaps the most pleasant to shoot of them all. A photographer must in some ways be an intruder but I was put so much at ease that I felt almost embarassed when I got to the second roll. Shooting was in daylight on the roof of her pretty, feminine cottage in Rome.

16

BRITT EKLAND

Swedish actress, internationally famous not least for her marriage to Peter Sellers and her associations with other leading international names. Britt is probably the easiest person to photograph that I have ever come across — she has a gloriously photogenic face and, armed with the self-confidence such knowledge brings, absolutely loves being photographed and is splendidly relaxed.

She has lately enjoyed additional success as a writer of 'fiction'.

This picture taken for *Vogue* was set in the grounds of my home, Shugborough, in the springtime.

TESSA DAHL

Born in 1957, Tessa Dahl is the daughter of the celebrated
Norwegian short-story writer, Roald Dahl, and the internationally acclaimed American actress, Patricia Neal.

The eldest of four children, Tessa looks startlingly like her
beautiful mother but has inherited characteristics from both
sides of her family. She took what was intended to be a brief
sabbatical from school when she was sixteen to appear in a
film in Nova Scotia starring Cloris Leapman, but when the film
was over saw little point in her abandoned education. A brief
foray into the antique world followed and she then moved on
to London where she was much escorted by, amongst others,
Peter Sellers and Hywel Bennett. She finally moved in with
Julian Holloway, son of the famous music-hall comedian,
Stanley Holloway, and father of her daughter, Sophie.

After her parting from Julian, Tessa worked as a journalist
writing Ms Dahl's Diary for the *Tatler*. On a trip to America in
the summer of 1980 to generate copy for her column, she met
Bostonian business man, James Kelly, and, at the time of
writing, they are to be married within six weeks.

At least five foot eleven, Tessa has immense natural ease and
poise; as Nigel Dempster once said: 'She is incapable of a
graceless movement,' and there is no nonsense about wearing
flat shoes. She also has remarkable bone structure and a face
which remains quite unmarked by a mode of living which
would bring most people to their knees with exhaustion
within hours.

LESLEY-ANNE DOWN

I had wanted to photograph Lesley-Anne Down ever since I saw her in her role as the beautiful niece in 'Upstairs Downstairs', the ITV television series. She also appeared in *Death On The Nile* (1978) and *The Betsy* with Laurence Olivier.

Lesley-Anne began modelling before she was thirteen years old and at fifteen was described in the press as 'the most beautiful teenager in Britain'.

I think she is, without question, the most attractive English actress to emerge in the last decade and I greatly looked forward to the photographic session. It transpired that she had had only three hours sleep the night before and she was distinctly weary but, obviously, lack of sleep does not in any way affect her appearance.

MARELLA OPPENHEIM

Sometimes there is only one obvious choice of a picture after a session. In this case I found it very difficult to choose as Marella's natural ability to work in front of a camera and response to direction were remarkable. A string of pearls can be a great prop.

ANOUSKA HEMPEL

Born in New Zealand of Russian and Swiss parents. Her first husband Constantine Hempel, by whom she has two children, was killed in a car crash in 1973 but with his encouragement she had begun to model and then act. She landed a small role in a James Bond film and then a part in the television series 'Zodiac'. In 1978 she married the actor Bill Kenwright and is now married to Mark Weinberg, the financier.

Diminutive, with huge eyes, Anouska is an active business-woman running her own hotel, the elegant Blakes, while continuing with her acting career.

DEBORAH KERR

A British actress, born in Clydeside, with an illustrious screen career stretching back forty years. She starred in such classics as *The Prisoner of Zenda* (1952), *From Here to Eternity* (1953), *The King and I* (1956) and *The Sundowners* (1960).

Avon Cosmetics commissioned me to photograph Deborah Kerr in a friend's house in London for the launch of one of their new products in 1980. It turned out to be a memorable occasion. We broke for lunch half way through the session and she so captivated us all that it was mid-afternoon before we resumed work again. Afterwards everybody in the crew asked to be photographed with her — something which has never happened before in my experience and perhaps gives some indication of what an engaging and fascinating woman Deborah Kerr is.

SARAH CLARK

Bayer Pharmaceuticals of Germany commissioned me to do a series based on Shakespeare's Seven Ages of Man. So here, not quite 'mewling and puking' is the result of the first age.

▷

JACQUELINE BISSET

Jacqueline is quite easily one of the nicest people I have ever worked with — warm, humorous and completely unspoilt by her phenomenal success. I met her first some years ago when she walked into a studio, where I was employed as an assistant, wanting some test shots, as she thought she would like to become a model. This picture was taken at that time.

She never did become a top model but, instead, went on to become one of the most sought-after British actresses in the world with film credits which include *Bullitt* (1968), *La Nuit Américaine* (1973), *The Greek Tycoon* (1979), *The Deep* (1979) and many others.

The bewitching sensuality of Jacqueline's looks have always appealed to me and I think this photograph, with its emphasis on eyes and mouth, has captured the nature of her attraction in the simplest way.

28

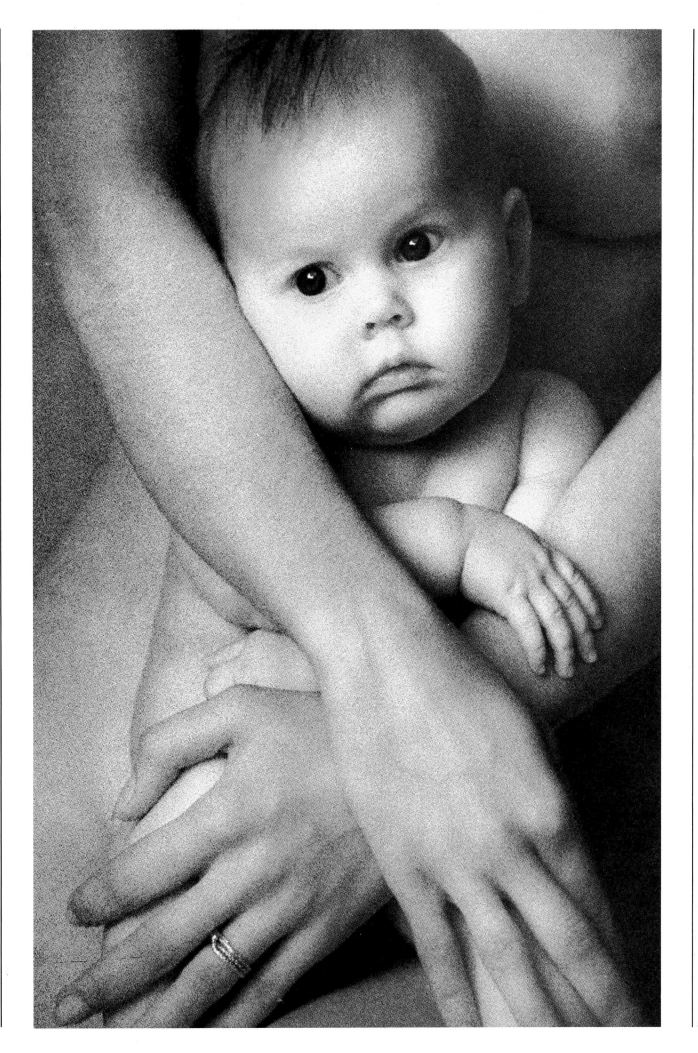

LADY SYLVY THYNNE

I was commissioned to photograph Sylvy's father, the Marquis of Bath, when I suddenly noticed his daughter and persuaded her to pose for me. One trick in photographing children is to use scale to emphasize the smallness of people and here it is done by surrounding her with a huge plant and an outsize dog.

KAREN PINI

Karen was Miss Australia in 1976. I was co-compering the Miss World contest with Sacha Distel when Karen was a competitor. She is a remarkable-looking girl and seemed all set to win but was narrowly beaten into second place by Miss Jamaica. After the contest was over I did some test shots of her and her pictures dominated the 1979 Unipart calendar.

Now a successful television actress in Australia I *still* think she ought to have won.

MRS DAVID BRUCE

Evangeline is the second wife of American diplomat, David Bruce, who was U.S. Ambassador to the Court of St. James in the late sixties.

Once voted one of the world's ten best dressed women, Evangeline has an affection for Britain and retains a flat in London. I photographed her at the U.S. Ambassador's residence in Regent's Park for *Harpers & Queen* using a very wide angle lens. I usually avoid this when photographing beautiful women but I wanted to give perspective to the room and use the dogs as a frame for her figure.

▷

SUE ELLISON

Just another test shot of a pretty girl taken in the sixties. I always thought that she should have tried to become a model but the prospect didn't seem to interest her. Nevertheless I include this for the simple reason that I am fond of it.

PRINCESS ELIZABETH OF TORO

Africa is the best source that I know of for women with marvellously long necks (q.v. Iman). On top of this particular long neck is a very active and intelligent brain. Princess Elizabeth of Toro is the daughter of the former Kabaka of Buganda. She qualified as a barrister and was the Ugandan minister for foreign affairs during President Amin's regime. She subsequently became a very successful model for *Vogue* in New York.

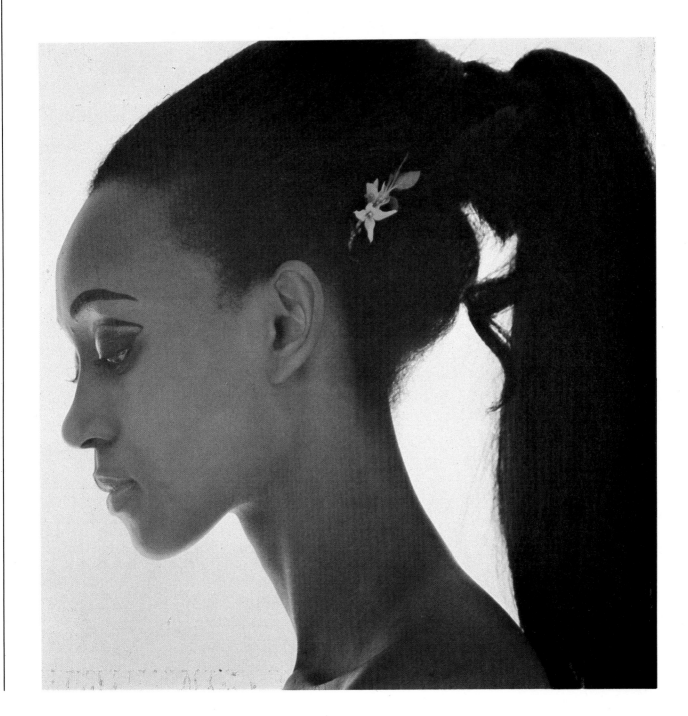

MARSHA HUNT

Marsha was in the original cast of the smash-hit musical, *Hair*, when it opened in London in the late sixties. I went to the première where all the stir about nudity on stage first began. Marsha, of course, appeared nude in the show so when I photographed her the very next morning, for American *Vogue*, she had to be shot this way. Subsequently, she became well-known as hostess of an outspoken London radio programme.

SARDINIAN GIRL

One day in Sardinia on location for *Vogue,* at the end of a session, I was walking past some vineyards when this girl walked straight past me. I took a quick shot of her and continued my walk but I was pleasantly surprised, when I processed the film later in London, by the result.

▷

THE COUNTESS OF SHELBURNE

When I was an assistant in a studio in Wilton Place in the sixties, I used to photograph Frances endlessly. She was cheerfully resigned to being used for practice purposes and as a stand-in and I produced hundreds of shots of her face, which has always seemed to me typical of the sixties with its large eyes and high cheekbones.

The Countess of Shelburne was born Lady Frances Eliot, daughter of the Earl of St Germans. She is married to the heir to the Marquis of Lansdowne.

JANE BIRKIN

This photograph was taken in Paris for American *Vogue* just after Jane's notorious record 'Je t'aime' had been released. The song was banned in countries all over the world and Jane's screen career — she made her debut in *Blow Up* — has been equally risque. However, it would have been hard to find anyone whose looks so belied her career.

She arrived with a basket containing little else besides her knitting and a clutch of quails' eggs looking to me exactly like a spectacular, but still demure, schoolgirl.

CELIA HAMMOND

I took this fashion photograph of Celia Hammond for the *Sunday Times* in the late sixties. Our major concern with this shot was to try to show the effect the designer had in mind and to display the sleeves with their butterfly-like appearance.

Celia Hammond was one of *the* models of the sixties. Along with Paulene Stone, Jean Shrimpton, Twiggy and perhaps one or two others she was in extraordinary demand for magazine and newspaper work — and, like them; she was a joy to photograph. With one proviso, though. A great lover of cats, both wild and domestic, she flatly refused to wear or model animal furs, so if you have ever seen Celia wearing fur — it was fake.

PENELOPE TREE

Penelope was very probably the most widely known and successful American model of the sixties — due, in part, to her liaison with David Bailey.

She comes from one of those grand, rich, old Anglo/American families and has many eminent forebears. I met her first in Barbados when I was commissioned to photograph her father's palatial house, Heron Bay. She was about fifteen at that time and already gave promise of being a great beauty. Subsequently, I spent many happy weeks staying with her parents in their splendid town house on 79th Street, New York, and came to know the family well. On one occasion I can remember Penelope appearing for dinner in a mini-skirt made entirely of foxes' brushes (tails) and she seemed perplexed by her father's expostulations — he was a former Master of Foxhounds.

Penelope was perhaps the first to combine successfully the roles of society beauty and working model. Shown here with her grandmother, mother and sister, it is apparent from where Penelope inherited her outstanding looks.

DIANA RIGG

Intelligent and perceptive actress whose career has encompassed James Bond films (*On Her Majesty's Secret Service* (1969)), the television series, *The Avengers*, and many roles with the Royal Shakespeare Company amongst much else. Born in Doncaster, in the north of England, Diana trained at the Royal Academy of Dramatic Art and her first appearance on stage was as Natella Abashwili in *The Caucasian Chalk Circle* at the Theatre Royal, York. She is currently appearing in the Muppet film and writing her own book.

I photographed her specially for this book as the only previous photographs I had of her were taken for the *Radio Times*, featuring Diana as a nun, a prostitute and a failed actress. At that session she adopted each of these persons in quick succession, without make-up, within one hour.

LAURA
GIRL ON A ROCKING HORSE

This photograph of the great-granddaughter of Sir Walter de la Mare, shot for American *Vogue*, was taken in Hatfield House, the home of the Marquess of Salisbury. I was accused of not giving the clothes enough prominence — an easy fault when presented with such a setting. To have got any closer would have simply ruined the effect of the picture.

MRS RUPERT HAMBRO

At the time this shot was taken, Robin Butler, as she then was, was working as London editor of American *Vogue.* In the course of doing a series of women wearing capes, I simply asked her to ride around the park at my house in the country whilst I shot from the roof of a landrover — the only problem was that my brilliant idea didn't do too much for the cape.

MAUD ADAMS

I'd seen Maud Adams' face on the cover of almost every magazine I'd come across in both New York and Paris. I left the direction of hair and make-up entirely in her own hands as I was sure she would know exactly what to do. A native of Sweden, Maud Adams is far more than just a perfect cover girl. She speaks five languages and made her film debut with Beau Bridges in *The Christian Licorice Stone* (1971). This was followed by a series of films including *Rollerball, Man with a Golden Gun* and *Killer Face,* and among her current projects is the highly controversial *Playing for Time* with Vanessa Redgrave in which Maud Adams plays a Jewish prisoner in a concentration camp.

LADY SARAH ASPINALL

Sarah Aspinall, photographed here in 1967, at her wedding to Piers Courage, the brewery heir and Grand Prix racing driver who was so tragically killed. She then married casino proprietor and zoo owner, John Aspinall, and they have one child. This photograph was a test shot taken in the studio while I was experimenting with a new lighting set up.

LADY ROMSEY

This photograph of Penelope Eastwood was taken at her wedding in 1979 to Lord Romsey, at Broadlands, the home of the late Earl Mountbatten of Burma.

PRINCESS LUCIANA PIGNATELLI

Italian-born, Luciana Pignatelli's name has been associated with beauty and cosmetics for many years — and she has written a well-known book on the subject. Twice married and now divorced, she divides her time between New York and her house in London, where this was taken in the summer.

ANN TURKEL

Lovely American actress and model who first achieved fame by appearing constantly in American *Vogue*, for whom I photographed her on location in England, the Bahamas and Sardinia in the early seventies. Her first film role was in 1974 in *99 and 44/100% Dead*.

Ann is very tall and perfectly proportioned and I remember, on one occasion, meeting her in a New York nightclub and asking her to remove her shoes when I asked her to dance — so we could be on more even terms.

Ann is married to the actor, Richard Harris.

SUSAN HAMPSHIRE

Blonde, English actress perhaps best remembered for her role as Fleur Forsyte in the television serialization of 'The Forsyte Saga' for which she won the Emmy award for Best Actress of the Year. She has appeared in a huge variety of productions from *Wonderful Life* (1964) with Cliff Richard to numerous classical stage plays, television and film productions.

This photograph was taken in my studio and we chose the eighteenth century dress because she seems to have become immortalized in those kind of historic roles. It was a difficult session because the BBC were filming us to be shown on the Russell Harty show and we fell over each other all the time. In comparison to the subsequent TV show however, when one of my fellow guests beat Mr Harty about the head, it was a piece of cake.

BIANCA JAGGER

I first met Nicaraguan-born Bianca Pérez Morena de Márcias sitting on the floor at a crowded party in Manhattan and remember thinking at the time that I had never seen anyone before who possessed her kind of uniquely individual features. Some time later I gave Bianca away at her marriage to Mick Jagger — a wedding perhaps without parallel in its excitement, glamour and general show-biz razamatazz. This photograph was taken in Mustique in the Caribbean some years ago. She is unique — I have photographed many women the world over, many of them are alike but I have never met anyone who remotely resembles Bianca.

SYDNE AND LISA ROME

During an assignment in South Africa I worked with Sydne on a major fashion feature. An American actress, she had just completed the film *Just a Gigolo* (1978) with David Bowie, and she brought her sister along with her to South Africa — quite possibly to act as chaperone. At the end of one day's shooting, after a great deal of persuasion, I managed to win them both over to the idea of doing this double-head photograph. Always a difficult shot to pull off as it is likely to become too posed, I was pleased, nevertheless, with the way that these two lovely girls naturally fitted together.

CHANTAL D'ORTHEZ

This is one of a number of test shots I did of Chantal when she was considering modelling as a career. She is the daughter of the well-known actress, Moira Lister, who has been appearing in character roles on stage and screen for many years.

COUNTESS VANINI

Daughter of a theatrical agent and his actress wife, Vicky (née Tennant) married an Italian Count and nightclub entrepreneur, Peppo Vanini. Her husband owns nightclubs all over the world including Manhattan's most successful discotheque, Xenon.

I photographed her for *Vogue* choosing a black background to contrast with her long blonde hair and pale, translucent skin.

DEBBIE HARRY

Lead singer of the group, 'Blondie'.

Thanksgiving Day. New York. Nobody working. Nobody *will* work until suddenly the telephone rings and Debbie Harry's agent is on the line. 'She can come if you want her, but what about the colour of the clothes?' 'Dark,' I said, 'preferably black.' This is not the way it turned out, as is obvious.

CATHERINE OXENBURG

Catherine is the daughter of Princess Elizabeth of Yugoslavia and New Yorker, Howard Oxenburg. Catherine was due to go to Harvard this year to study Chinese, but she and her mother moved to New York where Catherine has since begun a modelling career. She has enjoyed this so much that she has put off going to Harvard University for a year and is obviously having a thoroughly successful time.

She arrived in the studio for the first beauty shot of a new magazine. In fact the shot was never used as the magazine didn't get off the ground. Apart from her wonderful eyes, Catherine has a strength in her face which, though, does not in any way detract from her feminity.

MIA FARROW

American born actress whose roles include the leads in *Rosemary's Baby* (1968), *John and Mary* (1969) and *The Great Gatsby* (1973). Here she is shown as Joan of Arc. The severe hair-style necessary for the role prompted me to design the photograph to emphasize the simple, waif-like quality of her face — a quality for which she is famous. It is very seldom that a stark, direct, head-on picture such as this works but a combination of bold lighting to enhance eyes and bone structure, together with a hard neckline, make this, I feel, a particularly arresting and dramatic portrait.

FIONA SUTCLIFFE

When I was asked to photograph the finalists for a hair styling competition this girl, from outside London and without any experience of modelling, appeared in the studio.

I include her in the book because I think she *is* amongst the most beautiful girls that I have photographed and also because, just once, I wanted to avoid the obvious temptation to include only 'names'.

THE LATE MRS PAUL GETTY

This photograph was taken at Paul and Talitha's house in Marrakech, Morocco, for American *Vogue* in the late sixties.

Talitha was a great hostess and used to hold enormous house parties to which the 'jet set' of the sixties flocked. Wild and flamboyant even by the standards of the time, Talitha's parties were fabled and many of them took place on the roof shown in the picture and lasted for days on end.

I photographed her here with Paul in the background showing Talitha draped, as usual, in some of the beautiful, bizarre clothes that she loved to wear.

Tragically, she died at an early age.

ANOUK AIMEE

Photographed here in Morocco during the filming of *Justine* (1969) in which she co-starred with Michael York and Dirk Bogarde. As an actress she is perhaps best known for her role in *Un Homme et Une Femme*, the 1966 film produced by Claude Lelouch which became an international box office success and for which Anouk was nominated for an Oscar.

KATE BUSH

Weird, wonderful and extremely popular singer whose unique style of singing and presentation on stage and screen has carved her a considerable niche in the pop world over the last few years. I thoroughly enjoyed photographing Kate. She came to my studio (with the Indian Headdress) and was completely happy to cooperate in every way with the make-up artist and me. She's an entertainer down to her fingertips and has a very strong sense of 'image' which makes a photographic session with her much more of a 'production' with everybody having great fun working together to produce the finished shot. She's diminutive and lively, with a fascinating, mobile face and reminds me nothing so much as a bright, beautiful little bird.

IMAN

The possessor of the longest neck in the world (q.v. Princess Elizabeth of Toro). Iman, born in Mogadishu, Somalia, was discovered by the photographer, Peter Beard and became a top model with *Vogue*. She took her first step from modelling into films when she appeared in the film, *The Human Factor*, starring Nicol Williamson which was released in Britain in 1980. This movie was made from the novel by Graham Greene and was partly filmed on my estate.

JOANNA LUMLEY

Joanna, British model and actress, was one of the first models I worked with when I embarked on my career as a fashion photographer. She had the miserable job of modelling swim-wear which entailed her standing in the Serpentine (the lake in Hyde Park, London) in mid-winter.

Since then not a year has passed without our working together including assignments in Mauritius, Toronto and South Africa. Joanna became very well-known to the public when she secured the role of Purdey in the television series 'The New Avengers', a series which was equally beneficial for her predecessors, Diana Rigg and Honor Blackman. Subsequently she has acquired something of a reputation for being very good at intellectual panel games on television.

This photograph was commissioned by Cartier in 1978 for a *Vogue* promotion.

LADY ANNUNZIATA ASQUITH

The daughter of Lord Oxford and Asquith, Annunziata is as academically gifted as she is beautiful. She read History at Somerville College, Oxford and now works as a researcher for films and television. She models very rarely and only for a well-known clothing store.

LISA TAYLOR, ANNA ANDERSON
AND EVA VOORHIS

These three girls are all from the Ford Model Agency in New York. Lisa Taylor (above) and Eva Voorhis (overleaf right) are American by birth but Anna Anderson (overleaf left) was born in Rome, of Norwegian parents, and began her modelling career in Paris. But, as any fashion photographer knows, most really good models have crossed the Atlantic. All these girls are in their twenties but they have an elegance and self-assurance well beyond their years.

ANNABEL HODIN

Before she became a professional model, Annabel came to the studio one day when I had just had a cancellation. I simply put her behind a bathroom window, splashed water over it and shot the picture from outside. Since then she has continued to model with considerable success.

MRS SIMON KESWICK

The daughter of Major David Chetwode, Emma married Far-East trader, Simon Keswick, whose family founded Jardine Matheson, the great Hong Kong trading company. She was sent to my studio by *Vogue* to be photographed for a spread on young English beauties during the late sixties.

She appeared shy, almost diffident, which doesn't help a sitting in the least, but I felt that her eyes had a fascinating intensity and matched so well her beautifully-proportioned face.

LULU DE LA FALAISE

This photograph was taken at Lulu's wedding to Desmond Fitz-Gerald, Knight of Glin, in 1966. Lulu is the daughter of the Marquis de la Falaise and the granddaughter of Sir Oswald Birley. I was commissioned by *Vogue* to go to the wedding and I rather treasure this photograph, though I would have liked to have photographed her mother and grandmother with her — each of them in her own way looked stunning. Most photographs of Lulu are the epitome of today's fashions and trends but this, oddly, appears pleasantly dated.

NATALIE WOOD

I have sometimes chosen early photographs of people for this book as they tend to be more flattering but Natalie Wood has aged so wonderfully well that I went to her house in Beverly Hills for a completely up to date picture though I had many earlier photographs to choose from. Her husband, Robert Wagner, was there and produced excellent Californian wine as we looked through an enormous cupboard crammed with clothes. This pair are notable for having divorced and then married each other again. A former child actress, Natalie's films include *Happy Land* (1943), *Rebel Without a Cause* (1955) *Bob, Carol, Ted and Alice* (1969), and she is perhaps best known for her role as Maria in *West Side Story* (1961).

PAULENE STONE

One of the great models of the sixties, she was married to the late Laurence Harvey. We have worked on numerous assignments together in Mexico, Sardinia and all over Europe, and I have invariably found her dependable, professional and utterly reliable — to the extent that I use half the film on her that I would on anyone else. She has terrific red hair but I chose this black and white picture because it seems to illustrate the natural elegance which I believe contributed so much to her success. She now lives in Los Angeles and is married to restauranteur, Peter Morton.

MRS CHRISTIAAN BARNARD

She is married, of course, to Doctor Christiaan Barnard, the pioneer of heart transplant surgery. This photograph was taken in Marbella on assignment for a South African magazine, *Fair Lady*. The feature was to show personalities modelling clothes rather than professional models and the shot was taken in the grounds of a large hotel called Los Monteros.

Very dark, long-necked and elegant Barbara Barnard is one of those lucky women for whom any clothes seem to have been specifically designed and she made a marvellous model.

SUSIE COELHO

Every photographer needs his luck. When I arrived at Sonny Bono's magnificent hilltop house in Beverly Hills, where he lives with Los Angeles' most exotic model, Susie Coelho, it was about ten minutes to sundown and the light was incredible. I asked Susie to collapse more or less where she stood and allowed the sun to come into lens to create a slightly flared effect. Apart from back lighting the subject this softened the general effect of the picture and, I thought, admirably suited her sultry looks.

SAMANTHA EGGAR

British-born actress who studied fashion design and entered drama school. Sir Cecil Beaton, photographer and designer, gave her her first professional role in his production, *Landscape with Figures*. She then appeared in the BBC television series, 'Rob Roy' which she left eventually to join a Shakespeare repertory company. She made her name in films co-starring with Terence Stamp in *The Collector* (1965) at which time this photograph was taken. Her other film credits include *Walk Don't Run* (1966), *Doctor Dolittle* (1967) and *The Molly Maguires* (1969). She also starred with Yul Brynner in the television series, 'Anna and the King'.

This, admittedly very dated, picture was taken in Kent on the set of *The Collector* during a lunch break. It was the first of many stills jobs I have done on feature films.

OLIVIA NEWTON-JOHN

I first met Olivia on an assignment to photograph Susan George for *Playboy* in Los Angeles. Susan brought Olivia along with her and she at once caught my eye. English-born but brought up in Australia, she looks like a particularly stunning version of the girl next door: slim, petite, healthy and athletic.

This photograph was taken from a set for *Harpers & Queen* at my house in the country and seems in pleasant contrast to the slick image created for her in her highly successful movies.

Olivia co-starred with John Travolta in the box-office success *Grease* (1978) and with Gene Kelly in *Xanadu* (1980).

SARAH HUTTON

Before marriage Sarah was Sarah Cubitt, a member of the building family who built much of Belgravia in London (including Eaton Square, Eaton Place and Belgrave Square) in the nineteenth century. She is the ex-wife of the advertising executive, David Hutton.

I decided to photograph Sarah especially for the book because her fresh, English looks particularly appeal to me. It is nearly always easier to take beauty photographs in controlled or studio conditions than outside. However in the case of Sarah Hutton I felt that some movement would help the picture, and this was made considerably easier by having the luck to choose a beautiful spring day. Thus we were able to produce what may appear to be something of a reportage shot. A nice change.

THE LATE LADY ELIZABETH
VON HOFMANNSTHAL

Considered by many to be the most beautiful Englishwoman of her generation, Lady Elizabeth was persuaded by *Vogue* (for whom her daughter, Arabella, was then working) to pose for this slightly diffident portrait. It is a strange and daunting feeling to be face-to-face, camera in hand, with someone whose beauty is so striking that you feel you can only produce something merely adequate as a portrait, as flattering them would seem to be quite impossible.

CASSANDRA HARRIS

Cassandra is an actress and was most recently seen in the James Bond movie, *For Your Eyes Only* (1981) with Roger Moore and Topol. Born in Australia, Cassandra followed a stage and screen career in that country and hosted her own live TV chat show. When she came to this country she did a number of TV plays and theatre work and toured with the National Theatre. She is currently working on the prestigious BBC series about Nancy Astor.

MARIAN LAH

This photograph of Marian, an American-born model, was taken on an Avon advertising shoot. I was struck by the symmetry of her face which was emphasized by the lighting — for obvious reasons cosmetic photographs have to be very carefully lit. We used her hands to add to the flowerlike nature of the picture and to give it the feel of a tulip. Her association with John Swanell, probably the most promising of young English photographers, may have helped her to become one of the most sought-after models currently working in Europe.
On the other hand, of course, she may have helped him.

JOAN COLLINS

Sultry, sexy British actress who has appeared in dozens of international films including *The Stud* (1979). She is shown here in her London home dressed in, and surrounded by, silver. I decided to show her like this, amid her collection of art deco, as I felt it reflected her enduring glamour and beauty. Joan is one of the few people that I have photographed who can be said to embody the word 'glamour' in its most unadulterated, old-fashioned sense. A genuine 'femme fatale'.

LADY LIZA CAMPBELL

Daughter of the Earl and Cathryn, Countess of Cawdor, Lisa was brought up in the incredibly beautiful and fascinating Cawdor Castle in Scotland. This photograph was taken during a shoot for the *Tatler* but was more intended for a test shot for a possible career in modelling.

▷

VICTORIA PRINCIPAL

The beach at Malibu (suggested by Victoria) provides a different location for this shot; she had even booked a room by the beach in which to be made-up and have her hair done. It was one of those miraculous days with the smog just beginning to clear and the sun to burn through that produces perfect photographer's light. A crowd gathered to watch but Victoria did not seem deterred, but rather encouraged, by the impromptu audience.

Bouncy, bright, athletic, the daughter of an Air Force sergeant, she, like Mary Crosby, has become famous for her role in the television series 'Dallas', as Bobby Ewing's wife, Pam. She lives in Beverly Hills and is married to actor, Christopher Skinner, whom she met on the 'Dallas' set when he made an appearance in the programme.

KITTY TANEN

Tall, languid, self-assured daughter of the film director,
Howard Hawks, Kitty lives in Santa Monica with her film
executive husband, Ned Tanen. I went to their home in
Beverly Hills to take this photograph and, on arriving, noticed
the jacussi in the garden. I thought it would be ideal to use in
the shot to emphasize Kitty's long neck. Once top of a list of
ten pretty socialites, Kitty used to work in the film industry
herself as an agent for writers and editors in California. She is
now learning to be an architect.

THE COUNTESS OF LICHFIELD

My wife, Leonora, included in this book despite her strong opposition.

JEAN SHRIMPTON

English model, 'The Shrimp', who almost certainly possessed the most photographed face of the sixties. She was *the* cover-girl of all time and achieved something of a record in having her picture on more magazine covers in one week than anyone has done before or since. She was 'discovered' by David Bailey and it is still a debatable question as to who made whom famous.

Jean Shrimpton was a great model. She had a rare ability to make any clothes she wore seem as though she owned them. The session from which this photograph was taken involved twenty-seven lingerie shots for American *Vogue* which she did for me in just two days. Anyone who has worked with models will know that this is an exceptional feat.

SINGAPORE GIRL

One of the plum photographic jobs is to be picked to do the Singapore Airline's advertising or their annual calendar and they commissioned me in 1978. I was issued with two genuine air stewardesses, not merely models posing as such, and I tried to find a situation which might be considered the absolute antithesis of the Orient and all its associations. We went to the Cotswolds for a country picnic, to Buckingham Palace for a shot with the Guardsmen and, finally, we posed her in the back of a London taxi cab. This, the last, was rejected in favour of another English scene but I liked it the best.

MADAME SUKARNO

An oriental beauty who was married to President Sukarno of Indonesia. Petite and feminine, Madame Sukarno is really the epitome of what Westerners regard as lovely in oriental women.

I met her in Paris once and suggested that, were she ever to find herself in Britain, she should look me up and I gave her my address in the country. On arriving at Heathrow some months later she gaily hailed a taxi and gave the driver the address. I think she was a little surprised to find herself, two-and-a-half hours later, in the depths of the Midlands with a considerable fare on the meter.

Japanese by birth, when speaking English she has a very endearing diction and is likely to get her 'Lolls Loyces' confused with her 'Lange Lovers!'

BARBARA PARKINS

Canadian actress perhaps best known for her role as Betty Anderson in the long-running television series 'Peyton Place'. She starred in *Valley of the Dolls* (1967) and co-starred with Orson Welles in *The Kremlin Letter* (1969). She studied dance from childhood and still attends dance classes regularly.

MRS JANE STEVENS AND PANDORA STEVENS

This photograph was taken as part of a series on mothers and daughters for *Vogue*. Located at their home in Hampshire, the clothes now seem extraordinarily dated though it is only ten years since this photograph was taken.

MRS RUPERT LYCETT GREEN

Daughter of Sir John Betjeman, she was photographed here in the sixties for *Queen* magazine. Now mother of five children, and with four books and two television documentaries to her credit, Candida and her husband breed racehorses in Wiltshire. Her husband also owns a well-known menswear shop in Savile Row where I bought everything I wore in the sixties.

MRS JOHN NUTTING

Born Diane Kirk, she was an extremely popular and successful debutante who married Earl Beatty, son of the late Admiral Beatty, in the 1950s. This photograph was a chance snap, taken after I had been photographing her children as a private commission, at Chicheley Hall, a beautiful eighteenth-century manor house belonging to Lord Beatty in Bedfordshire. Diane subsequently, in 1973, married barrister, John Nutting, son of former Tory minister, Sir Anthony Nutting, who resigned from the Macmillan government over the Suez crisis.

SUZY KENDALL

Suzy was born in Derbyshire, England, and studied at Derby College of Art. Her father, who owned a chain of interior-decorating shops, influenced her choice of career as a fabric designer. When he died she turned one of the shops into a restaurant and sold it eighteen months later as a going concern in order to try modelling.

Christopher Miles, brother of the actress Sarah Miles, spotted Suzy's screen potential and cast her in his comedy *Up Jumped A Swagman*. Since then she has appeared in a number of films including *To Sir With Love* (1967), *Up The Junction* (1968) and *The Betrayal* (1969). In partnership with the former model, Pat Wellington, she has started her own cosmetic business. This photograph was taken for *Vogue*.

BARONESS THYSSEN

Brazilian-born, Baroness Denise Thyssen (née Shorto) married Baron Heini Thyssen Bornemisza, son of the Ruhr steel magnate and owner of Europe's finest art collection. Somehow I have never associated blonde hair with South American women, yet here is someone whose hair would not suit her if it was any other colour. I photographed the second half of her wedding — the first half was spent locked in the boot of a car by a competitive journalist.

▷

BARONESS ANDREA VON STUMM

I photographed Andrea as part of a series of tests for the advertising of a well-known clothing store. Not surprisingly, she got the job. She has what appears to be an arrogant look which can be enormously helpful in front of a camera. Tall and elegant with striking eyes, she has the kind of looks not often found in English girls.

110

LYNSEY DE PAUL

The *Telegraph* magazine sent me to shoot some pictures of singer, Lynsey de Paul, at her house in North London. While we were looking for possible locations in her house I noticed the tiny piano — apt and attractive — so it seemed quite natural to put it in the shot.

▷

ALANA STEWART

In 1972 I was having lunch in the Beverly Hills Hotel in California when Alana walked in to the dining room with her fiance, George Hamilton. As soon as I saw her I was determined to photograph her but it was not until two years later that the opportunity arose after a chance meeting in a London nightclub.

Born in Texas, Alana is a strikingly beautiful woman which perhaps explains why she is now married to that celebrated connoisseur, Rod Stewart.

JERRY HALL

A Texan whose name has been romantically linked with Mick Jagger, she was also once engaged to Bryan Ferry. Jerry Hall is the epitome of the new style of model — very tall (over six foot), statuesque and possessed of an astonishing grace. Like Alana Stewart she has marvellous hair and perfect teeth, and is wonderful to photograph. She needs no direction from the photographer and my only worries were technical ones. She wanted to wear something grand and glamorous and found these dresses in Paris where I shot these pictures.

ANNALISA BROMLEY

This portrait of Annalisa, the wife of the electronics millionaire, Martin J. Bromley, was taken in my studio. Although I had never met Annalisa before I found her spontaneous and easy to work with, and genuinely very beautiful.

PALOMA PICASSO

Having seen Helmut Newton's pictures of Paloma in both his recent books — and also because everyone told me that I *had* to include her in this book — I went to Paris just to do this shot. After one roll of film, a large tear rolled down her cheek — more make-up, then more tears. Evidently it was nothing I had done or said, but simply a draught which somehow had this unfair effect.

Paloma is the daughter of the artist, Picasso, and designs jewellery which is marketed by the famous jewellery firm, Tiffanys, in New York.

MARY CROSBY

The girl 'who did it'. Daughter of Bing Crosby and his second wife, Kathryn, Mary shot to fame with her role as J.R.'s sexy mistress in 'Dallas', the successful American TV soap opera.

For some years Mary used to appear with her two brothers, her mother and father on Bing's annual TV Christmas show. She has had guest roles in 'Starsky and Hutch' and 'Dick Turpin' on television but, certainly, 'Dallas' has proved a unique and amazing vehicle of success for Mary and indeed for all its stars.

I took this photograph of her when she was over in Britain recently, working on a film. She has hair that seems to go on forever so it seemed only natural to make it the main feature of the shot.

FIONA LEWIS

The daughter of a lawyer, she was born in Westcliff-on-Sea in Essex. Having studied French at the University of Grenoble, she was encouraged to act by Roman Polanski and now her film credits include *The Fearless Vampire Killers* (1967), *Villain* (1971), and *Lisztomania* (1975). Her films seem to be largely of the horrific kind, which is surprising, as she is a gentle creature with a recently discovered talent for journalism.

MERYLL LANVIN

The wife of Bernard Lanvin of the famous French fashion house. I had seen Madame Lanvin at various gatherings in Europe and had always wanted to photograph her. When the opportunity came with this book I took several rolls of film, both in black and white and colour, but this simple setting in black and white seemed better than the colour shots I tried.

LADY ASHCOMBE

There is, I think, in American women an attitude to domesticity which sets them apart from their English counterparts. Because of this, *Queen* magazine ran a series in 1967 on American hostesses in London and Lady Ashcombe (then Mrs Dent-Brocklehurst) was understandably included. Neither quite a fashion nor a beauty picture, this photograph shows someone of singular poise in their own environment which, to my mind, is a natural way of photographing 'personalities'.

GAYLE HUNNICUTT

I first met Gayle when I was sent to Marbella in Spain to photograph her for a cosmetics advertisement. An American actress from Fort Worth, Texas, she has starred in many films including *The Wild Angels* (1966), *Marlowe* (1969) and *The Sellout* (1976). When I first met her she was married to the actor, David Hemmings (with whom she co-starred in *Fragment of Fear* in 1969) and she seemed every inch a typical Texan beauty complete with drawl. The only thing that has changed about her in the ensuing years is her accent — a vocal transformation from 'Texas drawl' to 'English lady' — but she is, if anything, even more beautiful.

She is married now to Simon Jenkins, former editor of the London *Evening Standard* and television presenter.

FAYE DUNAWAY

This photograph of Faye Dunaway, the American actress, was used for the cover of Britain's *Radio Times*. The BBC rang me one day to ask if I would be prepared to fly to New York and back in twenty-four hours to take a picture of her. Somewhat taken aback, I suggested that it would be much easier, and cheaper, if they commissioned an American photographer to take the picture. However, it seemed that patriotism prevailed at the BBC and so I flew to New York. A nerve-wracking few hours then ensued. Faye was one-and-a-half hours late arriving at the studio, leaving me with only enough time to take one roll of film while the taxi, summoned to rush me to the airport, ticked away outside — anyway, *Radio Times* used it.

Faye, who was born in Florida, became internationally successful with her lead role in the film *Bonnie and Clyde* (1967). Her many other films include *The Thomas Crown Affair* (1968), *Little Big Man* (1970), *The Three Musketeers* (1973), *Chinatown* (1974) and *Network* (1976).

MARISA AND BERRY BERENSON

No two sisters could look less alike and I have tried to photograph them as exact opposites, which I believe in some way reflects their personalities. I took Marisa's first ever professional photographs some years ago and, coincidentally, at the same time her sister came to my studio to apply for a job as my assistant. Berry then worked for three years in my dark room while Marisa became a top American model.

They are the granddaughters of the French couturier, Elsa Schiaparelli, and the great nieces of the legendary art historian and critic, Bernard Berenson. Marisa moved on from modelling to make her screen debut in *Death in Venice* (1972) and then appeared in *Cabaret* (1972) and *Barry Lyndon* (1975). Berry meanwhile married the actor Anthony Perkins who starred in *Psycho* (1960) as well as many subsequent movies.

EMMA AND JOANNA JACOBS

Daughters of the radio and television broadcaster, David Jacobs, who first went on the air during the Second World War and has since become a household name. Both girls began their careers as models but Emma has become an actress and appeared in several films including *The Stud* (1979). During the session at which I took this photograph, Lord Snowdon dropped in for a chat (it's a habit of photographers to 'pop in' to other photographers' studios). He caused, not surprisingly, considerable disruption — a hazard of the profession!

THE HONOURABLE
MRS SIMON FRASER

Photographed long before she married Lord Lovat's son, Virginia was never a model in the professional sense of the word but was much in demand for fashion photographs for American *Vogue*.

LESLIE CARON

French actress perhaps best remembered in the title role of *Gigi* (1958) and for her lead in *The L-Shaped Room* (1962). She was discovered by Gene Kelly and has followed an extremely successful career in light drama and comedy.

I have photographed her on several occasions, once with her daughter, but this soft, misty picture is my favourite. The effect was achieved by a process known as vignetting.

SOPHIA LOREN

Incredibly, this beautiful woman has been starring in films for nearly thirty years. Italian-born, married to producer Carlo Ponti, she has made scores of films from epics like *The Pride and The Passion* (1957), *El Cid* (1961), *The Fall of the Roman Empire* (1964) to comedies like *The Millionairess* (1961) and *Marriage Italian Style* (1964). She won an Oscar for her performance in *Two Women* (1961).

Since she was one of the people I considered indispensable for this book I made a quick flight to Paris just to photograph her. Like all beautiful women she is not really difficult to photograph — beauty bestows confidence and makes people relaxed in front of a camera. She came in to ask what clothes I wanted her to wear and disappeared to change. When she returned she simply sat down on a sofa and, really, there was nothing else to do. I did not need to move or pose her and two rolls of film and twenty minutes later I was in the taxi and on my way back to the airport.

What Sophia says of herself is true: her eyes *are* too wide apart, her neck too long, her mouth too wide. But add it all together and you get someone of whom Noel Coward once said: 'She should have been sculpted in truffles so that the world could devour her.'

KATE JACKSON

The only 'Charlie's Angel' who was a professional actress before the television series, Kate Jackson lives in Beverly Hills (where this photograph was taken), with her three Huskys chosen for the extraordinary colour of their light blue eyes. She met me in blue jeans, a denim shirt and bare feet and, most unusually, I didn't ask her to change as I felt her casual clothes suited her exactly.

VALERIE PERRINE

The sign on Valerie Perrine's front gate reads 'No Smoking' which I found a great deal more daunting than the four Great Danes who knocked me over as I arrived. Her house is enormous, even by Hollywood standards, and her rose garden is her one great passion and talking point. She is sensual, charasmatic and vivacious, and she has phenomenal energy. She rushed about making stronger and stronger cups of expresso coffee (a rare find in Hollywood) and then plied me with so much wine and cheese that it was difficult to remember what I was there for.

Born in 1946, her film credits include *Slaughterhouse Five* (1972), *Lenny* (1974) in which she played Lenny Bruce's wife, Honey, and her latest film *Can't Stop the Music* (1979) in which she stars with the US disco group 'The Village People'.

131

ANNE ARCHER

When I recently arrived in Los Angeles with a list of people to photograph, I asked everyone I met if there was anyone I had missed out. With one accord they all said Anne Archer. Soft spoken and gentle, she has the classic American face with a mass of luxuriant hair. It doesn't matter what angle you photograph her from as her face is so regular that all sides are equally good.

Born in Los Angeles, she recently married the actor Terry Jastrow and has one son from her previous marriage to businessman William L. Davis. She appeared in *Green Ice* with Ryan O'Neal, and in *Raise the Titanic* (1980).

DEBORAH RAFFIN

Daughter of the actress Trudy Marshall, who appeared in later Laurel and Hardy films, Deborah is a top model. Her film career began when she was spotted in a lift by a talent agent and, without even a screen test, was given the leading role in *40 Carats* (1973) playing Liv Ullman's daughter. Gregory Peck admired her performance and chose her to be in *The Dove* (1974) which he produced himself. She is married to producer Michael Viner.

SHAKIRA CAINE

I photographed Shakira Caine, Michael Caine's wife, in the garden of their house in the mountains behind Beverly Hills. Michael is an old friend of mine but tactfully kept away during the session although he was longing for news of London and home. Shakira, who was born in Guyana, is not a professional actress (despite her famous husband, and despite her non-speaking role with him in *The Man Who Would Be King*), but has her own career as a fashion designer. Her clothes were about to be introduced to the public when I was with them in the autumn of 1980 and she has just opened her own boutique in Los Angeles.

I first photographed the Caines when they became engaged and I noticed then Shakira's great natural dignity, easy carriage, poise and grace. She has the sort of face which is so perfect in itself that I yielded to the temptation here to come in close for a head shot and forego the rest of her — which is equally beautiful.

MRS RICHARD COOPER

I first met Janet Lyle, as she then was, at a dinner party in Lord Iliffe's house in the early sixties. I remember two things about that evening: the first was that we ate haddock mousse and the second was that I sat next to Janet. Why on earth I should remember the former is inexplicable but it would be entirely understandable if I did not forget the latter. Years later we started a boutique in New York together where we astounded passers-by by bumping along Madison Avenue in an aged London taxi cab which we used as a delivery van.

Forthright, down-to-earth and witty, Janet is a true Scottish beauty like her mother.

ALEXANDRA BASTEDO

Of Canadian, Italian and British descent, Alexandra was brought up in Brighton and is the mascot of the Royal Hampshire Regiment. Her first big break was her co-starring role in the television series, 'The Champions', and she has also appeared in a number of films including *Casino Royale* (1967). Quite apart from being unusually attractive, she has a dazzling array of academic achievements to her name.

She is the only lady I have ever known who can sit through five days of a test match without complaining.

This photograph was taken for *Spotlight*, the actors' directory.

CINDY BREAKSPEARE
MISS WORLD

In November 1976, Sacha Distel and I were asked to co-compere the Miss World competition at the Albert Hall. Apart from a near disaster when we left our radio microphones switched on during an interval when we were discussing the contestants in supposed privacy, all went reasonably well. Wonder Woman came fifth.

We took this shot of the winner the morning after the competition — no signs of hangover or reaction, though.

HELEN STEWART

Lovely, Scottish born wife of Jackie Stewart, the retired racing driver, who was three times World Champion and who was also, incidentally, at one time a champion Clay Pigeon shot into the bargain. I saw Helen at a party and asked her if I could photograph her. She said: 'Yes, but only if I can be dressed as Charlie Chaplin.' So that's what we did though, sadly, the famous moustache really didn't suit her so we had to omit it. In fact the choice of, if not bizarre, then certainly masculine clothes seems to create a more feminine and vulnerable impression than one might suppose.

LYNNE FREDERICK

The last wife of the late Peter Sellers whom she married at the age of twenty-two, she has recently married David Frost, the television personality.

Born in Middlesex, she left school when she was nearly sixteen to play a leading role in *No Blade of Grass* (1970). A year later she appeared as Tatiana in Sam Spiegel's *Nicholas and Alexandra* (1971) and later played Katherine Howard in the film version of *Henry VIII and his Six Wives* (1972). Her other films include *The Amazing Mr Blunden* (1972) and *Voyage of the Damned* (1976) with Orson Welles, Faye Dunaway and James Mason.

This picture was taken for *Vogue* when she was in her late teens.

MICHAELA CLAVELL

American-born daughter of the best-selling author, James Clavell, who wrote *Tai-Pan, Shogun* and also directed the films, *King Rat* and *The Last Valley* amongst others. Michaela came to my studio for some tests and I decided as soon as I saw her to include her in the book. I used her subsequently on a number of modelling assignments both in the studio and on location.

ANNA BJÖRNSDOTTIR
MISS ICELAND

On a trip to the Philippines to photograph President and Madame Marcos, the Miss Universe contestants were, by chance, my travelling companions. Miss Iceland was not among the winners of the competition but she caught my eye on the journey, despite the hottest competition which surrounded her, because of her absolutely classic nordic beauty. I used as much black in the photograph as I could to offset her hair and skin. She has since become a successful model both in London and New York.

CHRISTINA FERRARE

American actress and model, who first appeared in movies while still a teenager, co-starring with David Niven in *The Impossible Years* (1968). In the seventies she became one of the most famous faces in American advertising as well as on the covers of magazines and in fashion layouts. Sensationally good-looking, she has the ability to adapt her 'image' — from the girl-next-door to sexy femme fatale and back again. Married to John DeLorean, the couple live in Los Angeles.

JANE SEYMOUR

English-born actress who first achieved fame in the James Bond film *Live and Let Die* (1973). She appeared, more recently, in the film *Somewhere in Time* (1980) with Christopher Reeve and Christopher Plummer. We met when I was doing some commercial beauty photography and I was fascinated by her extraordinary hair which is exceptionally beautiful. Subsequently, I did this picture in the studio aiming to stress and highlight this feature, and I was particularly pleased with the smooth and uplifted line of the arm, hair and torso.

▷

TRACY REED

Daughter of Sir Carol Reed, the British film director, Tracy starred with Peter Sellers in Stanley Kubrick's film, *Dr. Strangelove* (1963). This photograph was the result of a commission from *Vogue* who wanted me to take pictures of various aspects of a new Knightsbridge store. Tracy was to be featured in different settings and this — in the health and beauty department which included a sauna amongst its facilities — seemed an appropriate pose. The window in the photograph fronted on to the street so, obviously, it was necessary to execute the picture with the utmost speed!

MARTHA MLINARIC

In the mid-sixties US *Vogue* commissioned me to take photographs for a feature they were doing on the young, romantic English (there was a lot of this kind of thing around then inexplicible as it may seem now). We didn't use professional models but young socialites of which Martha Laycock, as she was then, was one. The setting — Henley — was chosen because of all its associations with English summer, Edwardian elegance, strawberries and cream and soft breezes over the river. Rupert Lycett-Green is in the background.

Martha is married to David Mlinaric, a young decorator widely known in England, most particularly for his recent work on National Trust houses.

NICKY SHULMAN

This was a studio photograph taken for *Ritz* in 1979. Nicky is the daugher of the Canadian-born journalist, Milton Shulman, who is theatre critic and journalist with the *New Standard*, and his wife, Drusilla Beyfus, associate editor of *Vogue*. Nicky is at present reading English at Corpus Christi — one of the first women to take a degree at that college — and confines her modelling to the vacations at the moment.

▷

PERSIS KHAMBATTA

Persis was Miss India at one time but has lately achieved her greatest fame by appearing bald in the film *Star Trek* (1979). It's a considerable tribute to her beauty that she still looked stunning even without hair. This shot was one of many taken for no particular purpose in the late sixties and, even though it is dated, I still like it.

STEPHANIE GRAINGER

Stephanie Grainger was the perfect model for an idea I had of photographing people in their fantasy roles. She posed in five completely different parts — among them a space-age woman and a jockey — and, with her infinitely fluid and malleable face, adapted immediately and quite naturally to each one.

I first met her before she was a professional model and because of her peculiarly interesting face, infinite patience and sense of humour, have photographed her many times. The full-length is a previously unpublished picture.

HER MAJESTY
QUEEN ANNE-MARIE
OF THE HELLENES

My first royal commission, undertaken in 1964, was to photograph Princess Anne-Marie of Denmark shortly after her eighteenth birthday and a few days before she was due to fly to Greece to marry King Constantine of the Hellenes. I was living in somewhat reduced circumstances at the time and I recall, vividly, my acute embarrassment when, on taking off my jacket to start work, I discovered that the right sleeve of my shirt was missing. The King, who was present at the session, spotted the tattoo I have on my arm and exclaimed: 'Aha! Mr Burchett on the Waterloo Road.' He was right. Mr Burchett *had* done my tattoo — the King had visited him on a number of occasions too.

When I first saw Princess Anne-Marie I saw the truth of King Constantine's remark, reported in the *Daily Express* before they were married, that she was the most beautiful girl he had ever seen. She is particularly striking and elegant with looks that seem to go on getting better.

LADY SAMANTHA FEILDING

◁

My god-daughter, Samantha Feilding, daughter of the Earl and Countess of Denbigh, aged five. Part of the secret of photographing children is to put them in situations in which they feel completely natural, however artificial the situations themselves may be. We made a great game of dressing Samantha up in this dress which was part of a feature English *Vogue* were doing on children's fashions, and she entered into the spirit of it with enthusiasm. I think this photograph gives an idea of just how bewitching very small children canbe.

SUSANNAH YORK

British actress with a long list of film credits which includes *The Greengage Summer* (1961), *Tom Jones* (1963), *The Killing of Sister George* (1968), *They Shoot Horses, Don't They?* (1969) — for which she won a British Oscar — *Images* (1972) and *Conduct Unbecoming* (1975). Susannah went to RADA and paid for her tuition fees by working as a tourist guide in Switzerland. She then went on to study art in Rome and Florence.

So often cast as a 'typical Englishwoman' Susannah is a thoroughly nice person with a mobile, changeable face that is quite difficult to photograph well. I met her first in Morocco and subsequently photographed her in Spain on the set of the film *Duffy* (1968) which also starred James Coburn, James Mason and James Fox. This was just a snap, unposed, caught while relaxing between takes. She seems to be one of those people whom it is better to photograph that way than in a posed studio setting.

MRS DAVID BAILEY

I was returning from Mexico with David Bailey some years ago and, on changing flights at Paris, saw Marie sitting at the other end of the plane. I had worked with her in London so I introduced her to David Bailey — and, they got married.

David, whose taste in women is second to none, is also shown in this photograph — in an unusually subordinate position. Though, I think, that Marie who has legs that start at her shoulder-blades and the langorous, easy grace of a cat, seems to be able to cope with him.

Marie is a model and part Hawaiian and part Scandinavian.

TECHNICAL NOTE

As the contents of this book span several years with some photographs going as far back as 1964, the equipment used has varied considerably. Most of my early work was shot on Zenza Bronica, working in the studio, and the Nikon system was used whilst on location. Always at hand, however, was my trusted old Rolleiflex which could be used almost anywhere when everything else packed up.

After a major burglary of my studio in 1975, I reviewed the cameras available and changed systems to those of Olympus and Hasselblad — both of which have been used for those photographs specially commissioned for this book.

For the vast majority of these photographs shot in the studio, electronic flash by Balcar, Bowen and Broncolor has been used, although, when I first started, electronic flash was in its infancy and most of the very early ones were taken by Tungsten. This was produced by a very large bank of lights which I built myself and subsequently converted to flash. There are now many of these models readily available on the market though I still prefer my original design.

However, if it is available, I prefer to shoot with daylight for, at its best, it is undoubtedly without equal for beauty shots.

Films change as fast as cameras do and I generally tend to prefer comparatively high-speed films for my work in black and white. Irritatingly these are often discontinued or 'improved' just when I have really discovered how to get the most out of them. As far as colour is concerned, Kodachrome 25 remains my firm favourite though I use all types of Kodak colour film, often pushed 2 stops or more when on location.

All the black and white printing and processing is carried out in my own studio but, since the premises lack sufficient room for colour processing work, all this is sent to outside laboratories, one of which I have just started.